Dedication

To the men who served in my Section of the 219th Military Intelligence Detachment, II Field Force Vietnam, 1967-68:

Front Row:	W01 Bill Davies, CW2 Wilbur Wiley, Lt. Reynolds, Lt. Irvin Thomas
Second Row:	PFC Ralph Symmes, Sp4 Gary Moore, Sp4 Al Cilurso, Sp4 Dave Bong, Sp4 Tim Hoover, PFC John Blair
On Jeep:	Sp4 Ron Bauman, PFC Keith Horning, Sp4 John Werner, Sp4 Mel Petrie, PFC Dave Morris

Contents

TEXAS LORE Volume Eight

LONE STAR LEGACIES

by Patrick M. Reynolds

Published by

The Red Rose Studio
Willow Street, PA 17584

ISBN 0-932514-23-5

The Red Rose Studio publishes many other books by Patrick M. Reynolds including the Texas Lore collection and Big Apple Almanac. For a catalog, send $1.00 to The Red Rose Studio, The Town of Willow Street, PA 17584.

Printed in the U.S.A.

This map shows the location of most of the places mentioned in this book.

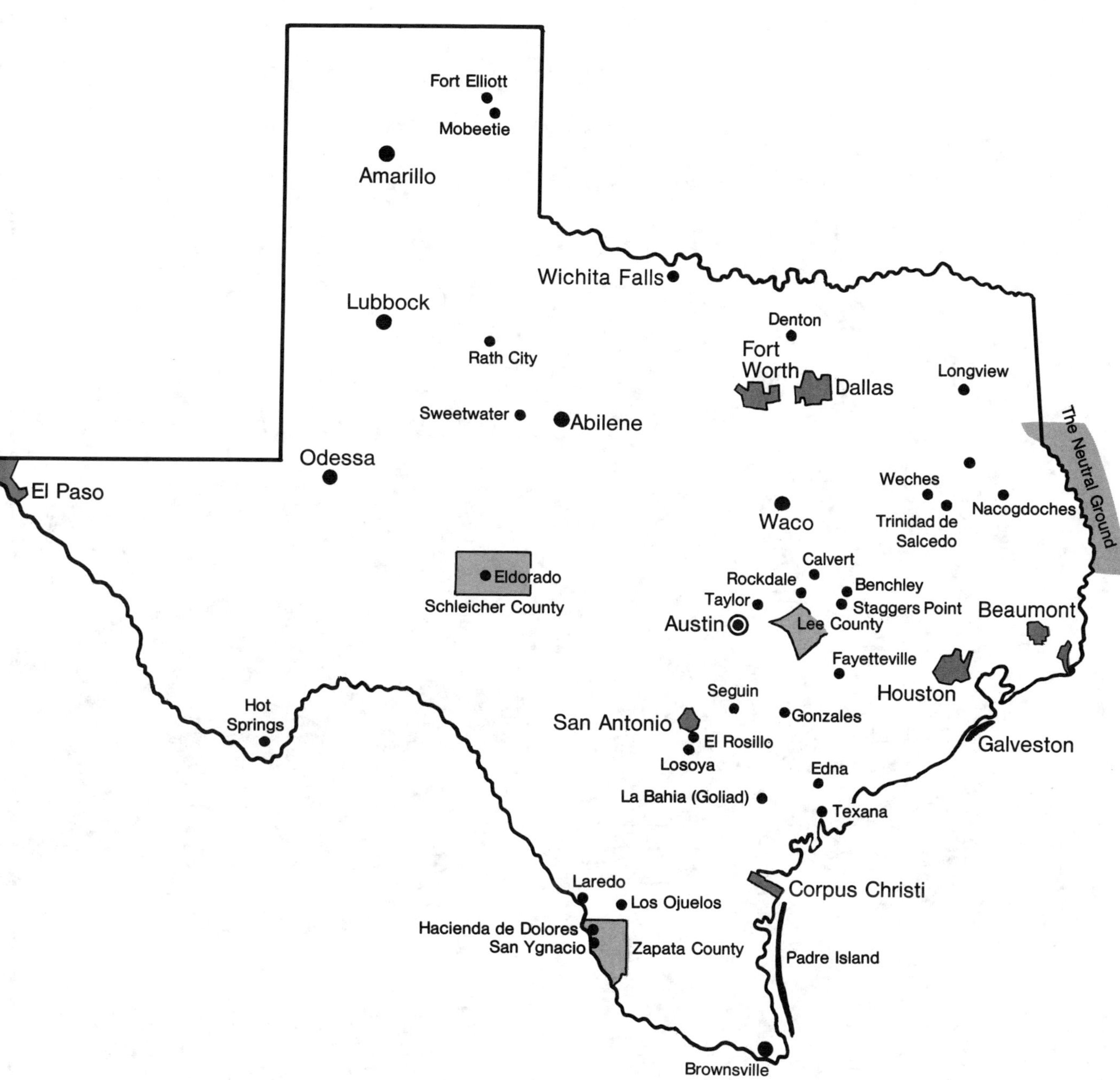

The Galleon Graveyard

PADRE ISLAND HAD LONG BEEN A GRAVEYARD FOR SHIPS DRIVEN AGROUND BY STORMS IN THE GULF OF MEXICO. ONE OF THESE DISASTERS OCCURRED IN 1553 WHEN A 20-SHIP SPANISH TREASURE FLEET RAN INTO A HURRICANE AND MANY OF THE SHIPS BROKE UP ON THE ISLAND.

OF SOME 300 SURVIVORS, ONLY TWO MANAGED TO ESCAPE THE KARANKAWA INDIANS AND HIKE BACK TO MEXICO.

THE SPANISH AUTHORITIES THOUGHT THE FRENCH WOULD TRY TO COLONIZE TEXAS AFTER LA SALLE'S BOTCHED EXPEDITION HERE. TO PREVENT THIS, DON ALONSO DE LEON, GOVERNOR OF THE AREA THAT INCLUDED TEXAS, LED AN ARMY OF SOLDIERS AND FRANCISCAN FRIARS TO WHAT IS NOW HOUSTON COUNTY.

THEY CONSTRUCTED A LOG MISSION IN MAY, 1690 AND CALLED IT SAN FRANCISCO DE LOS TEJAS BECAUSE THE SPANIARDS REFERRED TO THE LOCAL HASINAI INDIANS AS "TEJAS." LOCATED ON SAN PEDRO CREEK NEAR PRESENT-DAY WECHES, IT WAS

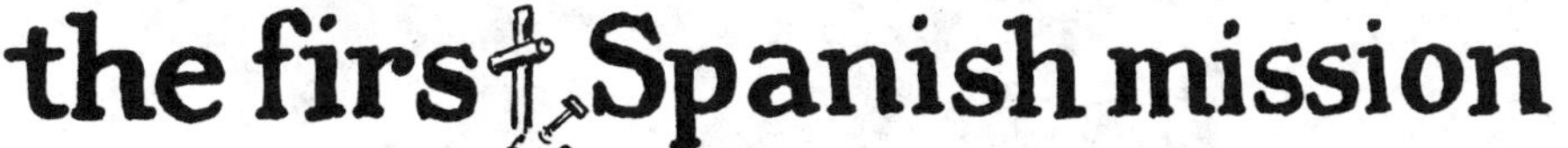

THREE FRANCISCAN FRIARS UNDER FRAY DAMIEN MASSANET AND THREE SPANISH SOLDIERS WERE LEFT AT MISSION SAN FRANCISCO DE LOS TEJAS (NEAR WECHES) IN 1690 TO CONVERT THE HASINAI INDIANS TO CHRISTIANITY AND CHASE AWAY ANY FRENCH EXPLORERS.
AT FIRST THE HASINAI WELCOMED THE SPANIARDS TO THEIR TERRITORY, AND THEIR CHILDREN ATTENDED
the first school in Texas.
HOWEVER, GOOD RELATIONS WITH THE INDIANS STARTED TO GO DOWNHILL WHEN THE SOLDIERS GOT OVER-FRIENDLY WITH SOME OF THE SQUAWS.

The Last of the First Mission

THE SPANIARDS AT MISSION SAN FRANCISCO de los TEJAS TRANSMITTED ALL SORTS OF DISEASES FROM MEASLES TO MUMPS TO THE INDIANS OF ITS NEIGHBORING VILLAGES. HAVING LITTLE OR NO IMMUNITY TO THESE AILMENTS, SOME 3,000 HASINAIS DIED BETWEEN 1690 & 1692.

THE NATIVES BEGAN TO AVOID THE MISSION LIKE A PLAGUE, LEAVING THE GARRISON WITHOUT ITS SUPPLY OF FOOD. THE SPANISH SOLDIERS REFUSED TO DO ANY FARMING.

IN 1692, FRAY MASSANET DECIDED TO BURN THE PLACE DOWN AND RETURN TO MEXICO. MORE THAN 20 YEARS WOULD PASS BEFORE THE SPANISH CAME BACK TO TEXAS.

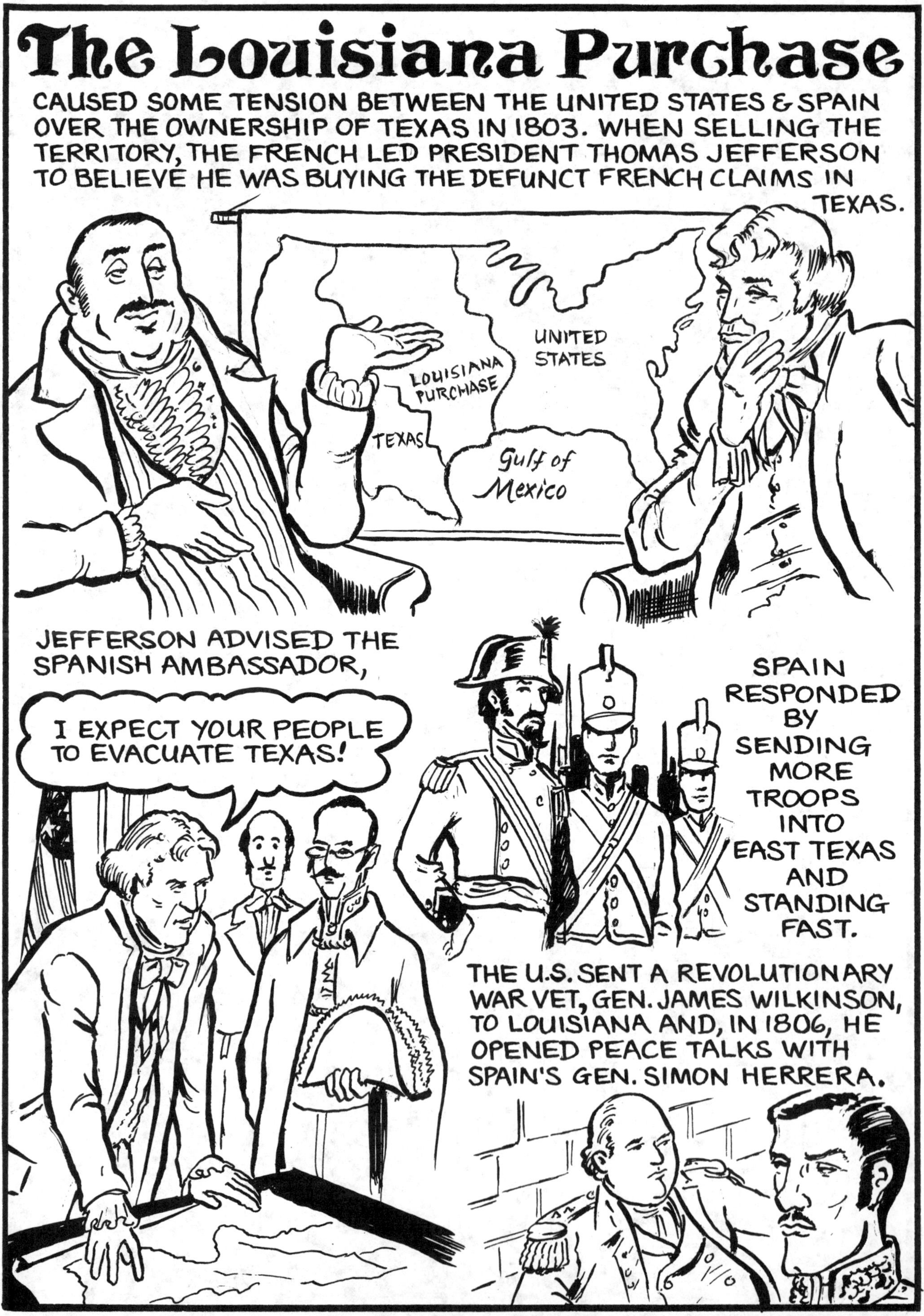

The Louisiana Purchase

CAUSED SOME TENSION BETWEEN THE UNITED STATES & SPAIN OVER THE OWNERSHIP OF TEXAS IN 1803. WHEN SELLING THE TERRITORY, THE FRENCH LED PRESIDENT THOMAS JEFFERSON TO BELIEVE HE WAS BUYING THE DEFUNCT FRENCH CLAIMS IN TEXAS.

JEFFERSON ADVISED THE SPANISH AMBASSADOR,

SPAIN RESPONDED BY SENDING MORE TROOPS INTO EAST TEXAS AND STANDING FAST.

THE U.S. SENT A REVOLUTIONARY WAR VET, GEN. JAMES WILKINSON, TO LOUISIANA AND, IN 1806, HE OPENED PEACE TALKS WITH SPAIN'S GEN. SIMON HERRERA.

WITH NO AUTHORITY TO NEGOTIATE FOR THEIR COUNTRIES, GEN. JAMES WILKINSON OF THE U.S. & SPAIN'S GEN. SIMON HERRERA AGREED TO ESTABLISH A BUFFER ZONE BETWEEN THE SABINE RIVER AND THE ARROYO HONDO CREEK.
LOUISIANA
TRINITY
BRAZOS
TEXAS
NEUTRAL GROUND
NEW ORLEANS
THE NEUTRAL GROUND,
AS IT WAS CALLED, SEPARATED THE LOUISIANA PURCHASE LANDS FROM THE SPANISH PROVINCE OF TEXAS IN 1806. FOR THE NEXT SIX YEARS THIS AREA WAS A HAVEN FOR THIEVES, KILLERS, SMUGGLERS, AND THE WORST DESPERADOS THE OLD BORDER HAD EVER KNOWN.

THE ENFORCER

WHEN LAW AND ORDER FINALLY DISINTEGRATED IN THE *NEUTRAL GROUND* IN 1810, THE U.S. ARMY SENT IN TROOPS TO GET RID OF THE TROUBLE-MAKERS. THE COMMANDER WAS A BRILLIANT BOSTON-IAN WHO GRADUATED THIRD IN HIS CLASS AT WEST POINT—**LIEUTENANT AUGUSTUS MAGEE.**

TO SHOW THAT THE UNITED STATES MEANT BUSINESS, LT. MAGEE HAD THE OUTLAWS HIS MEN CAPTURED TIED UP AND FLOGGED. SOON THE TROUBLE ENDED IN THE AREA.

DESPITE HIS GOOD RECORD, MAGEE WAS DENIED PROMOTION TO CAPTAIN. DISGUSTED, HE RESIGNED FROM THE ARMY IN 1812.

BACK IN LOUISIANA, MAGEE MET A REVOLUTIONARY GENERAL NAMED BERNARDO GUTIERREZ DE LARA WHO WAS TRYING TO RAISE AN ARMY TO OVERTHROW THE SPANISH RULERS OF MEXICO.

BERNARDO GUTIERREZ AND AUGUSTUS MAGEE PLANNED TO INVADE TEXAS AND LIBERATE IT FROM SPANISH RULE. WITH INDUCEMENTS OF $40 A MONTH AND A LEAGUE OF TEXAS LAND, MAGEE SOON ENLISTED A FEW HUNDRED AMERICANS, CAJUNS, MEXICANS, AND INDIANS IN WHAT HE CALLED
the Republican Army of the North.
IN AUGUST, 1812 THE ARMY HEADED TO NACOGDOCHES, TEXAS.
REALIZING HE WAS HEAVILY OUTNUMBERED, CAPT. MONTERO, COM-MANDER OF THE SPANISH GARRISON IN THE TOWN, ORDERED A RETREAT TO SAN ANTONIO.
WITHOUT FIRING A SHOT, THE FILIBUSTER (LAND PIRATE) ARMY TRIUMPHANTLY RODE INTO NACOGDOCHES.

The Magee-Gutierrez Expedition

LEFT NACOGDOCHES, MARCHED WEST, AND REACHED THE TRINITY RIVER IN OCTOBER, 1812. THEY OCCUPIED A SPANISH VILLA, TRINIDAD DE SALCEDO IN PRESENT MADISON COUNTY, DECLARED TEXAS A REPUBLIC, AND HOISTED A GREEN FLAG AS ITS EMBLEM.

THEIR NEXT OBJECTIVE WAS THE SPANISH STRONGHOLD OF BEXAR (SAN ANTONIO) BUT, AS THEY WERE CROSSING THE COLORADO RIVER, A ROYALIST DESERTER WARNED MAGEE THAT GOVERNOR SALCEDO WAS WAITING WITH 1,400 TROOPS AT THE GUADALUPE RIVER.

The Siege of La Bahia

THE MAGEE-GUTIERREZ EXPEDITION BYPASSED GOVERNOR SALCEDO'S AMBUSH AND RODE 120 MILES TO LA BAHIA (NOW GOLIAD). CAUGHT OFF GUARD, THE 160 SPANISH DEFENDERS FLED IN TERROR. INSIDE, THE REVOLUTIONARIES FOUND THE SPANISH COMMISSARY AND PAYROLL.

AS MAGEE WAS PAYING HIS MEN WITH GOOD SILVER FROM THE SPANISH TREASURY, GOV. SALCEDO AND GEN. HERRERA SURROUNDED THE PLACE WITH 800 TROOPS. A FOUR MONTHS' SIEGE ENSUED.

The Mysterious Death of Magee

COL. MAGEE DIED AT LA BAHIA (GOLIAD) IN FEB., 1813. SAM KEMPER TOOK HIS PLACE AS MILITARY COMMANDER OF THE MAGEE-GUTIERREZ EXPEDITION OF **FILIBUSTERS**—MEXICAN AND AMERICAN ADVENTURERS WHO TRIED TO LIBERATE TEXAS FROM THE SPANISH EMPIRE

IN MID MARCH, 1813, GOVERNOR SALCEDO LIFTED THE SIEGE ON LA BAHIA & RETREATED TO SAN ANTONIO

GUTIERREZ, KEMPER, AND 800 OF THEIR MEN FOLLOWED THE RETREATING SPANIARDS. ON MARCH 29, NINE MILES SOUTH OF SAN ANTONIO, KEMPER'S FILIBUSTERS RODE INTO AN

AMBUSH AT EL ROSILLO.

THE FILIBUSTERS CHARGED AND BROKE THROUGH THE SPANISH LINE, THEN PUSHED ON TO THE WALLS OF SAN ANTONIO.

Prelude to an Atrocity

APRIL 1, 1813—SAN ANTONIO WAS SURROUNDED BY 800 FILIBUSTERS UNDER KEMPER AND GUTIERREZ.

ON KEMPER'S PROMISE OF SAFE PASSAGE FOR THE SPANISH TROOPS, GOVERNOR SALCEDO SURRENDERED.

GUTIERREZ DECLARED HIMSELF PRESIDENT OF TEXAS, THEN HE OKAYED A **SECRET PLOT** BY CPT. ANTONIO DELGADO TO EXECUTE THE OFFICERS.

ON THE NIGHT OF APRIL 2, DELGADO LED ABOUT 100 REVOLUTIONARIES TO THE PRISONERS' QUARTERS ON THE PLAZA AND ABDUCTED GOV. SALCEDO, GEN. HERRERA, AND 15 OTHER OFFICERS, AND MARCHED THEM OUT OF TOWN.

The Massacre at La Tablita

ON THE NIGHT OF APRIL 3, 1813 SOME 100 FILIBUSTERS (REBELS) UNDER ANTONIO DELGADO HERDED 17 SPANISH PRISONERS OF WAR, ALL OFFICERS, OUT OF SAN ANTONIO TO A PLACE CALLED *LA TABLITA*. HERE THEY TIED THE OFFICERS' HANDS AND...

WHEN WORD ABOUT THE MASSACRE REACHED SAMUEL KEMPER, MILITARY COMMANDER OF THE FILIBUSTERS, HE IMMEDIATELY BROKE WITH "PRESIDENT" GUTIERREZ, THEN LED HUNDREDS OF VOLUNTEERS BACK TO THE UNITED STATES.

THE MASSACRE ALSO LED TO THE OUSTING OF GUTIERREZ AS "PRESIDENT" OF TEXAS. HE WENT BACK TO LOUISIANA.

ON AUGUST 4, GUTIERREZ WAS REPLACED BY JOSE ALVAREZ de TOLEDO.

Twilight of a Revolution

THE MAGEE-GUTIERREZ EXPEDITION BEGAN TO FALL APART IN AUG., 1813 WHEN HENRY PERRY TOOK OVER AS MILITARY COMMANDER AND JOSE TOLEDO BECAME "PRESIDENT" OF TEXAS. BOTH MEN INTENSELY HATED EACH OTHER.

MEANWHILE, JOAQUIN de ARREDONDO, COMMANDANT GENERAL OF NEW SPAIN'S EASTERN PROVINCES, LED A 2,000-MAN ARMY INTO TEXAS TO DRIVE OUT THE FILIBUSTERS.

ARREDONDO'S ARMY HALTED AT THE MEDINA RIVER. "PRESIDENT" TOLEDO WANTED TO DEFEND THE NORTH BANK AND MAKE THE SPANISH COME TO HIM, BUT PERRY REFUSED TO LISTEN.

HE STUBBORNLY LAUNCHED AN ALL-OUT ATTACK ACROSS THE MEDINA AT **LOSOYA**.

IT WAS EXACTLY WHAT ARREDONDO WANTED.

AUGUST 18, 1813 – THE FILIBUSTER ARMY SPLASHED ACROSS THE MEDINA RIVER SOUTH OF SAN ANTONIO AT LOSOYA. THE SPANISH GENERAL ORDERED A FEW OF HIS COMPANIES TO FALL BACK AS IF IN A PANIC. THE AMERICAN, MEXICAN, AND INDIAN REVOLUTIONARIES GAVE CHASE AND QUICKLY FELL INTO
A TRAP.
GEN. ARREDONDO HAD SET UP A V-SHAPED AMBUSH. THE AMERICAN GROUP OF FILIBUSTERS UNDER HENRY PERRY STOOD AND FOUGHT UNTIL ALMOST ALL WERE KILLED.
THE MEXICANS AND INDIANS UNDER "PRES." TOLEDO TRIED TO ESCAPE TO LOUISIANA. ONLY A FEW MADE IT. THE REST WERE HUNTED DOWN AND KILLED.
THAT WAS THE END OF THE MAGEE-GUTIERREZ EXPEDITION.

One of the Wildest Incidents

IN THE EARLY SETTLEMENT OF TEXAS WAS THE **FREDONIA REBELLION.** IT BEGAN IN 1825 WITH THE ARRIVAL FROM MISSISSIPPI OF AN ARROGANT AND SHADY *EMPRESARIO* NAMED HADEN EDWARDS (RIGHT), AND HIS HOT-HEADED BROTHER, BENJAMIN.

THE MEXICAN GOVERNMENT HAD GIVEN **HADEN EDWARDS** A GRANT OF OVER 300,000 ACRES NEAR THE EAST TEXAS VILLAGE OF **NACOGDOCHES** ON WHICH HE PLANNED TO SETTLE 800 AMERICAN FAMILIES.

THERE WAS ONLY ONE PROBLEM...

PARTS OF EDWARDS' LAND GRANT WERE ALREADY OCCUPIED BY MEXICANS & AMERICANS, MANY OF WHOM HAD LEGAL CERTIFICATES TO THEIR LAND.

Haden Edwards' Ultimatum

THE MEXICAN GOVERNMENT DESIGNATED HADEN EDWARDS AN *EMPRESARIO*, GRANTING HIM 300,000+ ACRES IN EAST TEXAS ON WHICH HE COULD DEVELOP A COLONY.

Who's in Charge?
IN JUNE, 1826, WHILE *EMPRESARIO* HADEN EDWARDS WAS IN THE UNITED STATES ON BUSINESS, HIS BROTHER, BENJAMIN, TOOK CHARGE OF HADEN'S COLONY IN EAST TEXAS.
ON STEPHEN AUSTIN'S ADVICE, BEN WROTE GOVERNOR BLANCO A FULL EXPLANATION OF HIS PROBLEMS WITH THE "EARLIER" SETTLERS ON HIS BROTHER'S LAND GRANT.
BLANCO'S REACTION:
THIS LETTER SHOWS A LACK OF RESPECT FOR SUPERIOR OFFICIALS. THEREFORE...
I AM REVOKING THE EMPRESARIO CONTRACT AND EXPELLING THE EDWARDS BROTHERS FROM THE REPUBLIC OF MEXICO.
HADEN EDWARDS HAD SPENT SOME $50,000 BRINGING AMERICANS TO EAST TEXAS, AND MANY OF HIS COLONISTS ALSO HAD GONE TO GREAT EXPENSE. GOV. BLANCO'S ACTIONS MEANT WAR!

THE ANNULMENT OF HADEN EDWARDS' EMPRESARIO CONTRACT SENT HIS BROTHER, BEN, ON THE WARPATH. HE NEEDED ALLIES, SO HE MADE A TREATY WITH THE **CHEROKEES** WHO HAD MIGRATED INTO EAST TEXAS, BUT WERE DISGRUNTLED BECAUSE MEXICO REFUSED TO GIVE THEM ANY LAND.

UNAWARE OF THIS, BEN EDWARDS AND 30 OF HIS COLONISTS RODE INTO NACOGDOCHES ON DECEMBER 16 1826, SEIZED THE FORT, DECLARED INDEPENDENCE FROM MEXICO, AND PROCLAIMED

the Republic of Fredonia.

The Fredonian Rebellion
LASTED ABOUT SIX WEEKS, FROM MID DEC., 1826 TO LATE JAN., 1827.
AFTER PROCLAIMING THEMSELVES THE REPUBLIC OF FREDONIA, BEN EDWARDS AND 30 OF HIS COLONISTS HOLED UP IN THE FORT AT NACOGDOCHES AND FOUGHT THE LOCAL MILITIA.
EDWARDS ASKED STEPHEN AUSTIN FOR HELP. NOT ONLY DID AUSTIN REFUSE, BUT...
HE ASSIGNED 100 OF HIS AMERICAN COLONISTS TO COLONEL AHUMADA'S MEXICAN REGIMENT THAT WAS MARCHING ON THE REBELS. IN RETURN, AHUMADA PROMISED AMNESTY TO ANY FREDONIAN WHO SURRENDERED.
DEAR MR AUSTIN

The Fall of Fredonia
ON JANUARY 28, 1827, A FORCE OF 250 MEXICANS AND 100 OF AUSTIN'S COLONISTS ARRIVED IN NACOGDOCHES AND PREPARED TO STORM THE FORT AND CRUSH THE FREDONIAN REBELLION.
BUT WHEN THEY GOT THERE THE FORT WAS ABANDONED.
HOPELESSLY OUTNUMBERED AND DESERTED BY THEIR CHEROKEE "ALLIES," EDWARDS AND MOST OF HIS FOLLOWERS HAD FLED TO THE UNITED STATES.
THE FREDONIAN REVOLT CAUSED A SENSATION BACK EAST, WITH AMERICAN SYMPATHY ON THE REBELS' SIDE.
Baltimore American
200 Men Against a Nation
SECRETARY OF STATE HENRY CLAY ISSUED A STATEMENT TO THE MEXICAN AMBASSADOR.
THE UNITED STATES GOVERNMENT HAD NO PART IN IT.
A RESIDENT OF NACOGDOCHES SUMMED UP THE REBELLION,
THERE WAS NEVER A MORE SILLY, WILD... SCHEME!

BETWEEN 1829 AND 1834, EIGHT IRISH FAMILIES LED BY ROBERT HENRY LEFT ALABAMA AND SETTLED IN A WOODED AREA WEST OF PRESENT-DAY BENCHLEY IN ROBERTSON COUNTY. JAMES DUNN BUILT A FORT. TO REFLECT THEIR DETERMINATION TO SUCCEED, THEY USED THE GAELIC NAME FOR "STRIVER" TO CALL THE PLACE
STAGGERS POINT.
THE COMMUNITY WAS CONSTANTLY HARASSED BY INDIANS. ON NEW YEAR'S DAY, 1839, A WAR PARTY KILLED SEVERAL MEMBERS OF THE GEORGE MORGAN FAMILY.
NINE DAYS LATER, 70 WARRIORS ATTACKED ANOTHER HOME.
BENJAMIN BRYANT DECIDED TO GO AFTER THE INDIANS.

FED UP WITH RAIDS ON STAGGERS POINT IN ROBERTSON COUNTY, BENJAMIN BRYANT ORGANIZED A POSSE OF 48 MEN TO HUNT DOWN THE HOSTILE INDIANS IN JANUARY, 1839. FIGURING THEY HAD SUPERIOR FIREPOWER, BRYANT'S MEN ADVANCED ON LINE TOWARD THE WOODS WHERE THE INDIANS WERE HIDING.
SUDDENLY, AN OVERWHELMING WAR PARTY CHARGED FROM THE WOODS.
BRYANT'S MEN WERE CUT OFF FROM EACH OTHER AND ALL FOUGHT HAND-TO-HAND COMBAT. SOME ESCAPED, BUT BRYANT AND TEN IRISH-MEN FROM STAGGERS POINT WERE KILLED IN WHAT BECAME KNOWN AS
Bryant's Defeat.

IN 1750 JOSE VASQUEZ BORREGO LED SPANISH SETTLERS TO THE HACIENDA de DOLORES, A FEW MILES FROM THE PRESENT TOWN OF SAN YGNACIO ALONG THE RIO GRANDE IN SOUTH TEXAS.
MEANWHILE, VINCENT GUERRA WAS ESTABLISHING A SETTLEMENT FURTHER SOUTH. THUS, CIVILIZATION WAS BROUGHT TO WHAT IS NOW
ZAPATA COUNTY.
FROM THE TEXAS REVOLUTION TO THE MEXICAN WAR, BOTH TEXAS AND MEXICO CLAIMED THE AREA. DURING 1839-40, COL. ANTONIO ZAPATA AND OTHER RESIDENTS BATTLED GENERAL CANALES AND THE MEXICAN ARMY.
THE GUADALUPE-HIDALGO TREATY IN 1848 GAVE THE PLACE TO TEXAS. TEN YEARS LATER IT BECAME A COUNTY AND WAS NAMED AFTER COLONEL ZAPATA.

The Teeming Town of Texana

DR. F. F. WELLS AND HIS SISTER-IN-LAW, MRS. PAMELA PORTER, FOUNDED TEXANA IN 1832. IT SOON BECAME A BUSY PORT AND SEAT OF JACKSON COUNTY.

AROUND 1836, THE BROTHERS ALLEN OFFERED $100,000 FOR THE TOWN IN ORDER TO BUILD A GREAT CITY AND SEAPORT. THE TEXANA FOLKS REFUSED.

AS THE ALLENS RODE AWAY, THEY PREDICTED,

SURE ENOUGH, IN 1883 THE RAIL-ROAD BYPASSED THE TOWN AND EDNA WAS MADE THE COUNTY SEAT. EVERYONE MOVED AWAY AND TEXANA CEASED TO EXIST.

BY THE WAY, THE ALLENS DID START THEIR CITY—**HOUSTON.**

The Ghost Town of Los Ojuelos

THERE ARE SMALL SPRINGS IN WEBB COUNTY THAT SEEP WATER TO THE SURFACE WHICH THE SPANISH CALLED LOS OJUELOS, *THE SPRINGS.* JOHN S. "RIP" FORD AND HIS TEXAS RANGERS CAMPED HERE IN 1850 WHILE GUARDING THE SOUTH TEXAS TRADE ROUTE BETWEEN LAREDO AND CORPUS CHRISTI.

JOSE GUERRA, OWNER OF THE LAND, BUILT AN IRRIGATION SYSTEM FROM THE SPRINGS AND ENCOURAGED MEXICANS TO SETTLE HERE. BY 1860, LOS OJUELOS HAD A POPULATION OF ABOUT 400.

OVER THE YEARS LOS OJUELOS DECLINED AND IS NOW A GHOST TOWN ON PRIVATE PROPERTY.

Mooney's Bridge

IN 1856 JOHN MOONEY BUILT A ROAD FROM GONZALES TO SEGUIN. A MILE AND A HALF OUTSIDE GONZALES, HE ERECTED THIS TOLL BRIDGE TO CARRY THE ROAD ACROSS THE SAN MARCOS RIVER. IT WAS ONE OF TWO KNOWN COVERED BRIDGES IN TEXAS.

MR. MOONEY'S HEIRS SOLD THE BRIDGE TO GONZALES COUNTY IN 1879, AND IT REMAINED AS PART OF THE COUNTY'S ROAD SYSTEM UNTIL A STEEL TRUSS BRIDGE WAS BUILT NEXT TO IT IN 1902.

TODAY, THE COVERED BRIDGE IS GONE AND THE STEEL SPAN IS CLOSED TO TRAFFIC.

LITTLE DENMARK

SOME TIME IN THE 1860's, TRAVIS SHAW & JOHN HESTER TURNED UP IN DENMARK, ASKING IF ANYBODY WANTED TO MOVE TO TEXAS. A FEW DANES SAID YES, AND THE TWO TEXANS SOLD THEM LAND IN **LEE COUNTY.**

AT FIRST, ABOUT 20 DANISH FAMILIES CAME OVER, FOLLOWED BY MORE IN THE 1870's. MOST SETTLED IN AN AREA ABOUT EIGHT MILES WEST OF **LEXINGTON** WHICH BECAME KNOWN AS *LITTLE DENMARK*.

SOME OF THE **FIRST DANES TO** ARRIVE IN TEXAS WERE: PAUL PAULSEN, A CABINET MAKER; NIELS THOMPSON, A BRICKLAYER; & PETER JENSEN, A BLACKSMITH.

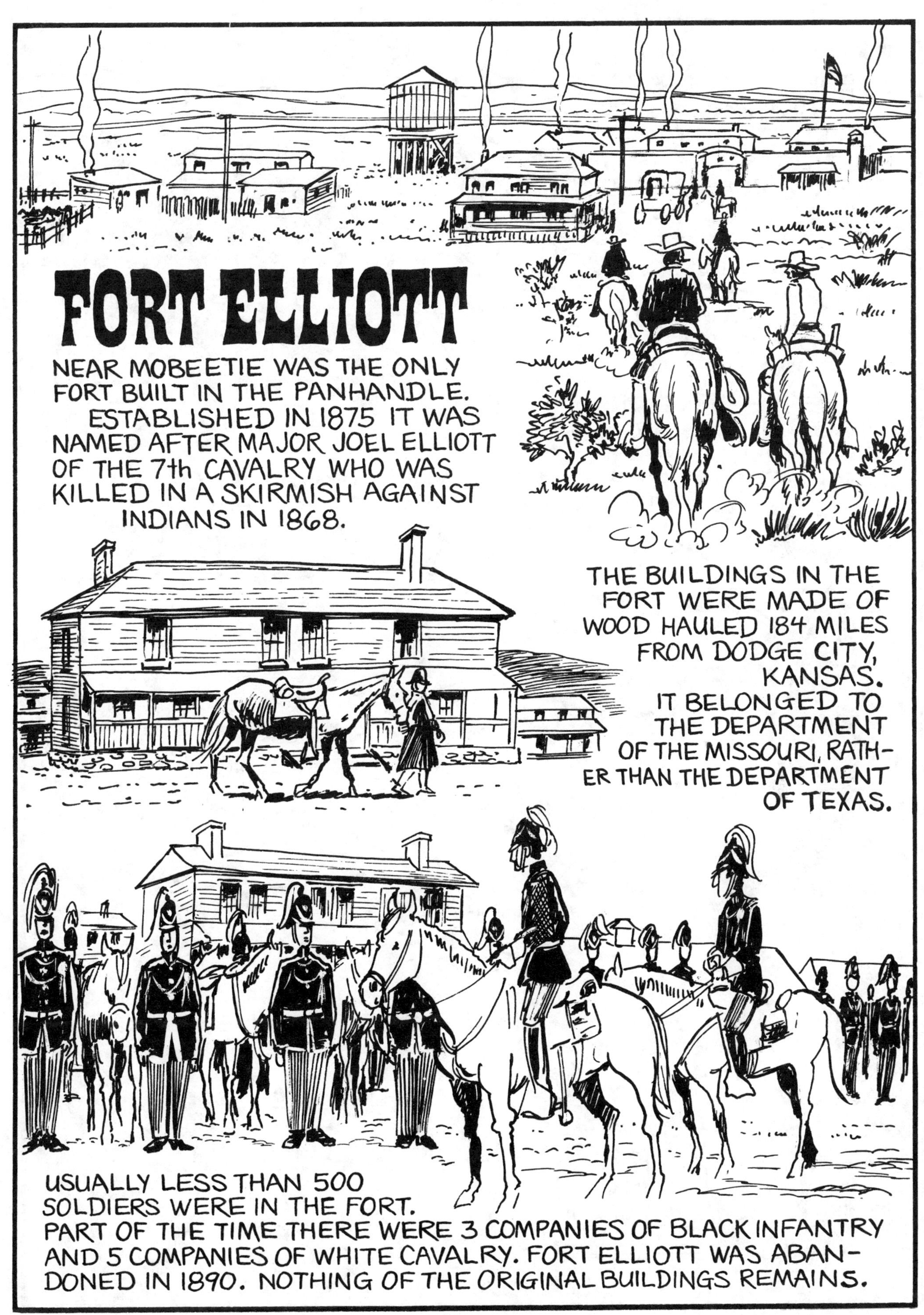
FORT ELLIOTT
NEAR MOBEETIE WAS THE ONLY FORT BUILT IN THE PANHANDLE.
ESTABLISHED IN 1875 IT WAS NAMED AFTER MAJOR JOEL ELLIOTT OF THE 7th CAVALRY WHO WAS KILLED IN A SKIRMISH AGAINST INDIANS IN 1868.
THE BUILDINGS IN THE FORT WERE MADE OF WOOD HAULED 184 MILES FROM DODGE CITY, KANSAS.
IT BELONGED TO THE DEPARTMENT OF THE MISSOURI, RATHER THAN THE DEPARTMENT OF TEXAS.
USUALLY LESS THAN 500 SOLDIERS WERE IN THE FORT.
PART OF THE TIME THERE WERE 3 COMPANIES OF BLACK INFANTRY AND 5 COMPANIES OF WHITE CAVALRY. FORT ELLIOTT WAS ABANDONED IN 1890. NOTHING OF THE ORIGINAL BUILDINGS REMAINS.

IN 1870, O.H. METHVIN DEEDED 50 ACRES TO THE SOUTHERN PACIFIC RAILROAD WITH THE UNDERSTANDING THAT THE RAILROAD WOULD BUY AN ADDITIONAL 50 ACRES, RUN A RAIL LINE THROUGH THE PROPERTY, AND BUILD A TRAIN STATION WITHIN THE TOWNSITE.
WHILE THE SURVEYORS WERE STANDING ATOP "CAPPS HILL" LAYING OUT THE TOWN, ONE ENGINEER REMARKED, "WHAT A LONG VIEW."
THAT INSPIRED MR. METHVIN TO NAME IT
LONGVIEW.
THE DISCOVERY OF OIL THERE IN 1931 MADE LONG-VIEW THE HUB OF THE EAST TEXAS OIL FIELD.
THE FIRST TWO GOVERNORS BORN IN TEXAS LIVED FOR A WHILE IN LONGVIEW:
JAMES HOGG, LEFT, AND HIS FRIEND THOMAS CAMPBELL.

THE SLAUGHTER OF BUFFALO BECAME THE MAIN INDUSTRY ON THE GREAT PLAINS IN THE 1870'S, AS THEIR HIDES SOLD FOR BIG BUCKS. THOUSANDS OF HUNTERS, SKINNERS, AND ADVENTURERS INVADED THE BUFFALO RANGE FROM THE KANSAS FRONTIER TO FORT CONCHO, TX.

OUT OF DODGE CITY, KS. CAME THE TOP BUYER OF BUFFALO HIDES, CHARLIE RATH, AND HIS IMMENSE WAGON TRAIN LOADED WITH KEGS OF POWDER, BOOZE, TOBACCO, AND OTHER GOODIES DEMANDED BY THE HUNTERS.

AROUND 1876 HIS ARMADA OF WAGONS AND 50 TO 60 BUFFALO HUNTERS PUSHED SOUTH THROUGH THE TEXAS PANHANDLE TO PRESENT-DAY STONEWALL COUNTY, FORGING WHAT WAS CALLED

THE RATH TRAIL.

IN 1876, CHARLIE RATH AND TWO PARTNERS NAMED REYNOLDS AND LEE TOOK A WAGONTRAIN OF MERCHANDISE TO THE DOUBLE MOUNTAIN FORK OF THE BRAZOS RIVER AT PRESENT-DAY STONEWALL COUNTY AND SET UP A TRADING POST AND BUFFALO-HIDE BUYING STATION.

THE TRADING POST ATTRACTED A COLORFUL COLLECTION OF HUNTERS, PROSPECTORS, AND DESPERADOS WHO STAYED IN A CLUSTER OF TENTS AND DUGOUTS KNOWN AS

RATH CITY.

RATH DID A BOOMING BUSINESS FOR TWO YEARS. WHEN THE BUFFALO WERE GONE IN 1879, RATH AND COMPANY PACKED UP AND LEFT. HIS CITY CEASED TO EXIST.

915
277
2084
190
190
ELDORADO
2596
Schleicher County
WAS CREATED IN 1887 AND NAMED AFTER GUSTAV SCHLEICHER, A LAWYER AND CONGRESSMAN FROM SAN ANTONIO.
AN EARLY LANDOWNER WAS WILLIAM L. BLACK, A CIVIL WAR BLOCKADE RUNNER. IN 1876 HE PAID 10¢ AN ACRE FOR 30,000 ACRES AND STARTED TO RAISE GOATS.
CHRISTOPHER COLUMBUS DOTY, THE COUNTY'S FIRST PERMANENT RESIDENT, DRILLED THE FIRST WATER WELL IN THE AREA, THEN PUT UP A WINDMILL. THIS ATTRACTED MORE SHEEP AND GOAT HERDERS.
TODAY, THE COUNTY SEAT, ELDORADO, HAS THE ONLY WOOLEN MILL IN THE SOUTHWEST WHICH WEAVES FABRICS FROM VIRGIN WOOL AND MOHAIR PRODUCED ON RANCHES IN WEST TEXAS.

The Oldest Family Band,

AS WELL AS **THE FIRST CZECH BAND, IN TEXAS** WAS THE **BACA BAND** OF **FAYETTEVILLE,** FAYETTE COUNTY. FRANK BACA ORGANIZED THE ELEVEN MEMBER ENSEMBLE IN 1882 AND IT QUICKLY GAINED WIDESPREAD POPULARITY.

PRIOR TO 1910, BEFORE THE AGE OF CARS AND RADIOS, AN IMPORTANT AMUSEMENT IN TEXAS' RANCH LANDS WAS THE
COWBOY DANCE.
THE MUSIC WAS USUALLY PROVIDED BY A LONE FIDDLER, AND EACH MAN WHO DANCED MADE A CONTRIBUTION TO THE MUSICIAN.
ENTIRE FAMILIES ATTENDED.
NO FORMAL ANNOUNCEMENT WAS MADE. A FEW WEEKS BEFORE THE DANCE, SEVERAL MEN TRAVELED AROUND & INVITED EVERYONE THEY MET. OFTEN, THE MOST POPULAR MEN AT THE DANCE WERE THOSE WHO RODE THE LONGEST DISTANCE TO THE DANCE. SOME RODE 40 MILES.

The Master Naval Tactician
THE SON OF SWISS IMMIGRANTS, EDWARD WALTER EBERLE WAS BORN IN DENTON IN 1864.
AFTER GRADUATING FROM THE U.S. NAVAL ACADEMY IN 1885, HE SERVED IN BOTH THE ATLANTIC AND PACIFIC FLEETS.
ON JULY 4, 1898, AMID THE SPANISH-AMERICAN WAR, EBERLE DIRECTED FIRE ABOARD THE *U.S.S. OREGON* AGAINST THE SPANISH FLEET AS IT TRIED TO BREAK OUT OF SANTIAGO BAY.
EBERLE DEVELOPED SMOKE SCREEN TACTICS, MINE-SWEEPING & MINE-LAYING TECHNIQUES FOR THE NAVY, AND HE WROTE THE FIRST MANUAL ON MODERN NAVAL ORDNANCE.
PROMOTED TO ADMIRAL, EBERLE WAS CHIEF OF NAVAL OPERATIONS FROM 1923 TO 1927.
HE DIED IN 1929.

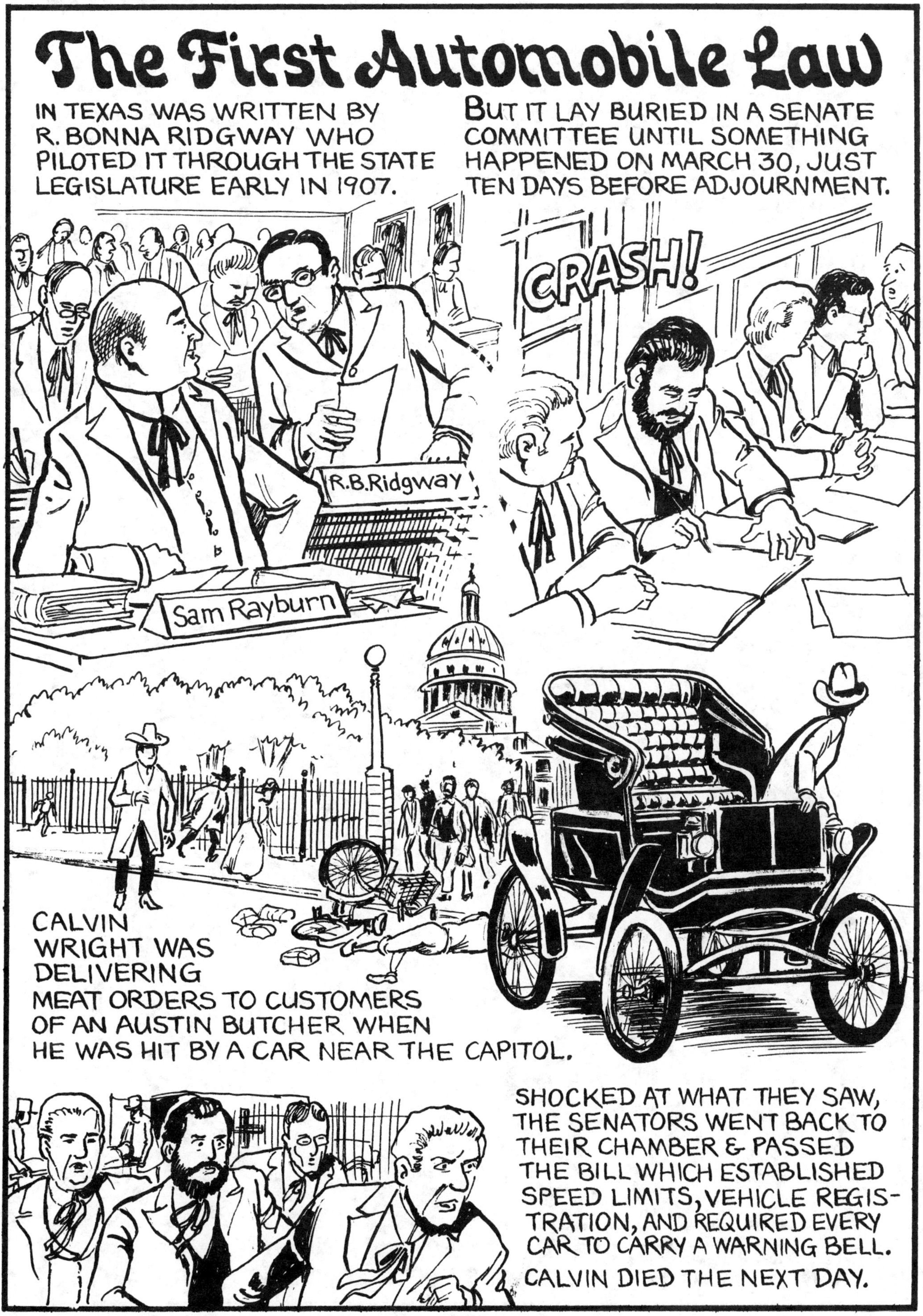

IN TEXAS WAS WRITTEN BY R. BONNA RIDGWAY WHO PILOTED IT THROUGH THE STATE LEGISLATURE EARLY IN 1907.

BUT IT LAY BURIED IN A SENATE COMMITTEE UNTIL SOMETHING HAPPENED ON MARCH 30, JUST TEN DAYS BEFORE ADJOURNMENT.

CALVIN WRIGHT WAS DELIVERING MEAT ORDERS TO CUSTOMERS OF AN AUSTIN BUTCHER WHEN HE WAS HIT BY A CAR NEAR THE CAPITOL.

SHOCKED AT WHAT THEY SAW, THE SENATORS WENT BACK TO THEIR CHAMBER & PASSED THE BILL WHICH ESTABLISHED SPEED LIMITS, VEHICLE REGISTRATION, AND REQUIRED EVERY CAR TO CARRY A WARNING BELL.

CALVIN DIED THE NEXT DAY.

The First Supermarket

FRANKLIN P. DAVIS OPENED A FOOD MARKET ON SAN JACINTO ST., HOUSTON IN 1916. IT WAS THE USUAL GROCERY STORE WITH A NEW ANGLE–UPON ENTERING, CUSTOMERS PICKED UP BASKETS AND **SERVED THEMSELVES.** THE MEAT WAS IN A COOLER IN THE CENTER OF THE STORE.

THE STORE CLOSED AFTER A FEW MONTHS BECAUSE OF MIS-MANAGEMENT, BUT THE CONCEPT OF SELF-SERVICE HAD BEGUN.

WHILE WORKING ON A CENTRAL TEXAS RANCH IN 1903, BILL PICKETT WAS ABOUT TO HAVE HIS HORSE GORED BY A STEER. THE BLACK COWBOY QUICKLY LEAPED FROM HIS SADDLE AND...
GRABBED ITS HORNS. THEN HE BIT THE COW'S UPPER LIP AND JERKED HIS HEAD, THROWING THE ANIMAL TO THE GROUND. ANOTHER COWBOY RUSHED OVER AND TIED ITS LEGS. THUS WAS BORN THE ART OF
BULLDOGGING!
HIS BOSS, LEE MOORE OF ROCKDALE, DECIDED THAT BILL SHOULD GO INTO SHOW BIZ.

BILL PICKETT BROUGHT HIS UNIQUE STYLE OF STEER WRESTLING TO THE *MILLER BROTHERS WILD WEST SHOW* IN 1905. OVER THE NEXT 15 YEARS HIS ASSISTANTS INCLUDED WILL ROGERS AND TOM MIX.
BILL GOT THE IDEA OF THROWING A STEER BY BITING ITS UPPER LIP AFTER WATCHING A BULLDOG CONTROL A COW THE SAME WAY. HENCE THE TERM *BULLDOGGING*.
THE DUSKY DEMON,
AS HE WAS BILLED, HAILED FROM TAYLOR, TEXAS. BILL WAS TRAMPLED TO DEATH WHILE BREAKING HORSES ON THE MILLERS' 101 RANCH IN 1932.
FORTY YEARS LATER, BILL PICKETT BECAME THE FIRST AFRO-AMERICAN TO BE INDUCTED INTO THE COWBOY HALL OF FAME.

BLACK ATHLETES WERE KEPT OUT OF BIG LEAGUE BASEBALL UNTIL 1947. NEVERTHELESS, ONE OF THE GAME'S FINEST PITCHERS WAS
ANDREW "RUBE" FOSTER.
BORN 1879 IN CALVERT, TEXAS, HE QUIT SCHOOL AFTER 8th GRADE TO PLAY PROFESSIONAL BASEBALL FOR THE WACO YELLOW JACKETS. FRANK LELAND DISCOVERED HIS TALENT DURING A GAME IN HOT SPRINGS AND RECRUITED FOSTER FOR HIS CLUB IN CHICAGO.
Lelands
MR. FOSTER TRIED TO IMPROVE THE LOT OF BLACK PLAYERS. HE STARTED THE NEGRO NATIONAL LEAGUE IN 1920 WITH CLUBS FROM KANSAS CITY TO INDIANAPOLIS, AND OFTEN SPENT HIS OWN MONEY TO KEEP SHAKY FRANCHISES ALIVE.
UNION GIANTS
UNION GIANTS
"RUBE" BROKE WITH LELAND IN 1910 AND TEAMED UP WITH A WHITE TAVERN OWNER TO FORM THE CHICAGO UNION GIANTS.

The Sweetwater Swatter
LEW JENKINS OF SWEETWATER STARTED BOXING IN CARNIVALS WHEN HE WAS A SCRAWNY 15 YEAR-OLD. HE BEAT ALL COMERS INCLUDING A FEW 200 POUNDERS.
EVERLAST
NINE YEARS LATER, ON MAY 10, 1940, JENKINS KNOCKED OUT LOU AMBERS IN THE THIRD ROUND TO WIN THE WORLD LIGHT-WEIGHT CHAMPIONSHIP.
THE SWATTER HELD THE TITLE FOR 19 MONTHS. HE RETIRED AT AGE 34 AFTER LOSING A TEN ROUND DECISION TO CARMEN BASILIO IN 1950.
JENKINS CLAIMED HE NEVER TRAINED FOR A FIGHT.

KEEP ON STROKIN'
ALFRED R. "RED" BARR
WAS A GREAT SWIMMING COACH AND ENERGETIC PROMOTER OF SWIMMING FOR ALL AGES IN TEXAS.
BARR COACHED SWIMMING FROM 1947 TO 1971 AT SOUTHERN METHODIST UNIVERSITY IN DALLAS, AND HIS TEAMS WON 17 SOUTHWEST CONFERENCE CHAMPIONSHIPS. FIFTY OF BARR'S SWIMMERS AT S.M.U. WERE ALL-AMERICANS.
COACH BARR DIED IN 1971 AT THE AGE OF 63.
THE OLYMPIC SIZED POOL AT S.M.U. WAS NAMED IN HIS HONOR.

Bob Wills and his Aladdin Laddies

WERE DOING A SATURDAY MORNING RADIO SHOW FROM THE KEMBLE BROTHERS FURNITURE STORE IN FORT WORTH IN 1930. BUT THE COUNTRY WAS MIRED IN A DEPRESSION, AND WILLS WAS WORRIED THAT THE ALADDIN LAMP CO. WOULD CANCEL HIS SHOW.

SHOWN ABOVE FROM LEFT: HERMAN ARNSPIGER, GUITARIST; TRUETT KIMZEY, ANNOUNCER; MILTON BROWN, SINGER; AND BOB WILLS.

TRUETT AND ED KEMBLE ASKED W. LEE O'DANIEL, GENERAL MANAGER OF THE BURRUS MILL & ELEVATOR CO., TO SPONSOR THE SHOW.

O'DANIEL DECIDED TO GIVE IT A TRY, AND THUS BEGAN ONE OF THE MOST POPULAR RADIO PROGRAMS IN THE ANNALS OF THE SOUTHWEST.

DURING HIS FIRST BROADCAST IN JANUARY, 1931 ON KFJZ, FORT WORTH, BOB WILLS JOKINGLY CALLED HIS BAND
"The Light Crust Doughboys."
THE NAME STUCK FOR THE NEXT TWO DECADES. THEIR DAILY SHOW OFFERED A VARIETY OF FIDDLE TUNES, BLUES, JAZZ, AND ABOVE ALL, POPULAR DANCE MUSIC.
HIS SPONSOR, THE BURRUS MILL & ELEVATOR CO., WAS IMPRESSED WITH THE SHOW, BUT NOT ENOUGH TO PAY WILLS AND HIS MEN A SALARY.
SO, WILLS WENT TO SEE W. LEE O'DANIEL, GENERAL MANAGER OF BURRUS.
EVENTUALLY, W. LEE HIRED EACH MUSICIAN FOR $7.50 A WEEK. THIS MEANT THAT AFTER THEY FINISHED THEIR MORNING SHOW, THEY PUT IN A FULL EIGHT HOUR DAY AT THE MILL. BOB WILLS DROVE A TRUCK.
BURRUS MILL & ELEVATOR CO.
FORT WORTH, TEXAS

THE LIGHT CRUST DOUGHBOYS SOARED TO FAME DURING THE HEYDAY OF RADIO WITH THEIR DELIGHTFUL BLEND OF BLUES, JAZZ, AND COUNTRY PLAYED WITH STRINGED INSTRUMENTS. THEIR LEADER, BOB WILLS, CALLED IT

WESTERN SWING MUSIC.

Wilbert Lee O'Daniel

DID NOT CARE MUCH FOR THE LIGHT CRUST DOUGHBOYS OR THEIR MUSIC ON THE RADIO SHOW THAT HIS FLOUR MILL SPONSORED IN FORT WORTH. THEN, ONE DAY IN 1931, BOB WILLS INVITED HIM TO SAY A FEW WORDS ON THE AIR.

FROM THEN ON, W. LEE WAS THE OFFICIAL HOST OF THE DOUGHBOYS.

O'DANIEL BOUGHT A BUS FOR THE BAND EQUIPPED WITH SIGNS AND A PUBLIC ADDRESS SYSTEM, THEN SENT THEM ALL OVER TEXAS TO PLAY AT SPECIAL OCCASIONS.

THE DOUGHBOYS BECAME GOODWILL AMBASSADORS FOR BURRUS FLOUR AND PROPELLED O'DANIEL INTO THE GOVERNOR'S OFFICE

"Pass the Biscuits, Pappy,"

WAS W. LEE O'DANIEL'S SLOGAN ON THE COUNTRY MUSIC RADIO SHOW HIS FLOUR COMPANY SPONSORED IN THE 1930's. THUS, "PAPPY" BECAME HIS NICKNAME.

IN 1938 "PAPPY" RAN FOR GOVERNOR. HIS PLATFORM WAS "UPHOLD THE TEN COMMANDMENTS, INDUSTRIALIZE TEXAS, AND PASS THE BISCUITS."

HE EASILY DEFEATED 13 OTHER CANDIDATES EVEN THOUGH HE WAS INELIGIBLE TO VOTE AT THE TIME BECAUSE HE REFUSED TO PAY HIS POLL TAX.

GOVERNOR "PAPPY" CONTINUED AS A RADIO FIGURE BY BROADCASTING EVERY SUNDAY FROM THE GOVERNOR'S OFFICE. HIS PROGRAM MIXED TAXES AND POLITICS WITH MOM, HOME, AND RELIGION.

Filling the Senator's Shoes

HIS LEGISLATIVE PROGRAM BOGGED DOWN. THE STATE WAS MIRED IN A $5 MILLION DEFICIT. NEVERTHELESS, GOVERNOR W. LEE "PAPPY" O'DANIEL WAS REELECTED IN 1940 BECAUSE HIS WEEKLY, HOMEY RADIO BROADCASTS MAINTAINED HIS POPULARITY.

IN 1941 "PAPPY" RAN FOR THE U.S. SENATE AGAINST 26 OTHER CANDIDATES FOLLOWING SEN. SHEPPARD'S DEATH. O'DANIEL NARROWLY WON THE DEMOCRATIC NOMINATION BY 1,095 VOTES OVER HIS CLOSEST RIVAL, A YOUNG CONGRESSMAN, LYNDON B. JOHNSON.

TEXANS GREW TIRED OF W. LEE'S FLAMBOYANT STYLE, BUT THE ESTABLISHMENT SUPPORTED HIS REELECTION TO THE U.S. SENATE IN 1942.

O'DANIEL DIED IN DALLAS IN 1969.

About the Author - Artist

Patrick M. Reynolds researches, writes, illustrates, and syndicates two state historical cartoons every week: *Pennsylvania Profiles* and *Texas Lore*, and one on New York City called *Big Apple Almanac*. Patrick attended Minersville (PA) High School, Pratt Institute, Brooklyn, NY, and earned a Masters of Fine Arts degree in Illustration at Syracuse (NY) University.

Texas Lore appears in the *Dallas Morning News*, the *Odessa American*, and the *San Antonio Express-News*.

Lt. Col. Reynolds is a veteran of the Vietnam War and a member of the US Army Reserves. Patrick and his wife, Patricia, live in the Lancaster County, Pennsylvania town of Willow Street with their two daughters, Kimberly Jo and Maria Alyssa, and their son, Thomas Patrick.